FAMILY BANK BLUEPRINT

STEPHANIE LENNON

For more information, contact Stephanie at:

Brooke Lennon, LLC dba MagniFI Your Life
1201 Sycamore Square Dr. #1313
Midlothian, Virginia 23113
Stephanie@ MagnifiYourLife.com

ISBN-13: 9798390443545

DEDICATIONS

To my Dear Husband and fellow banker.
We're doing something right!
Thou

~~

To my parents Art & Terri,
who imposed the *Brooks Bank*
upon their unsuspecting daughters.

Thanks for teaching us the value
of delayed gratification and holding firm
when we resisted every step along the way.

7 Catalysts for Change in our Home: Where We Began

1. **Finance 101.** What is money? Where does it come from? Where does it go? Nobody knows. The kids viewed credit cards as an infinite supply of funds.

2. **Saying Yes.** The children frequently asked us to buy stuff for them. Everyone got frustrated with "No."

3. **Household Participation.** The children weren't pulling their age-appropriate weight at home. It was time to engage them in the household labor force.

4. **Income.** The kids wanted the ability to earn and needed safe, age-appropriate ways to do so.

5. **Spending With Purpose.** Cash burned holes in little pockets. They wanted to spend it as soon as possible.

6. **Accounting.** Being unmarked, cash drove countless disputes over how much belonged to whom.

7. **Future Planning.** The kids needed to learn how to handle small change while they were young, so they could handle the big bucks when they're grown.

WHY YOU NEED A FAMILY BANK

You want to raise your kids to be kind, responsible, capable, successful adults. The kind of grown children who stand on their own two feet.

You strive to arm your children with the skills they need. Some training will come from the schools they attend. Other skills are survival based, so they can take care of themselves physically, in the civilized world and in the natural one. You teach them empathy and social awareness so they navigate human relationships with finesse. In short, you raise them to "adult" smoothly.

> **Are you teaching them enough about managing their money and constrained-resource decision making?**

An area of training that I see systemically lacking is personal finance. Schools have started teaching this – a little. Some parents teach it – and others don't. Society puts a damper on the discussion, where most circles consider it rude to discuss money too concretely.

Imagine seeing these posts in your social media feed:

"I got a $6,000 raise! At $132,000 now! Super psyched"

"Check out my new ride. Car pmts will b $775 fr 5 yrs. Hope I don't wreck b4 payoff LOLs"

"I'm struggling this month to make my $1100 rent payment. Hit me up with leads for part time work" [or *"Donate to my Go Fund Me!"*]

"My great aunt Sally died. I didn't know her at all, but she left me half a mill. Can you believe my luck?!"

"My student loan debt just hit $250,000. UGH."

When you imagine reading these, do you pity the poster? Are you jealous? Are you taken aback at the honesty? Would you post these?

Most people would more readily put their weight, cholesterol level, and blood pressure numbers online than their financial details. We shy away from sharing what we feel is intensely personal information.

Together, physical health and financial health correlate deeply to longevity and the quality of life during this lifespan. In the USA, a 14.6 year gap in life expectancy has been reported between the richest 1% of the male population and poorest 1%. Over fourteen years!! Amongst women, the gap is 10.1 years.[1]

Shouldn't we be discussing finances more openly, when our kids' lives depend on it? While this hush-hush protocol may be the culture we live in today, I'm concerned when these details are equally secret within families. My goal is to help you

---

[1] Chetty R, Stepner M, Abraham S, et al. The association between income & life expectancy in the United States, 2001–2014. JAMA. 2016; 315: 1750-1766

crack open the financial conversations in your home, specifically with your young children.[2]

Your goal is to raise kids who can independently manage their own households and finances. Who live 10-15 years longer on average in health and prosperity. Who do NOT call asking for money or boomerang home to live in your basement indefinitely. You must protect your nest egg to fund your retirement instead of their adult survival. If you have them plugged into indefinite economic life support, it drains your own.

If this scares you because you don't feel confident yourself, it's OK.

Setting up a Family Bank is not difficult, and you do not need to understand fancy Wall Street stuff to succeed.

Take it one piece at a time. Implement the elements that resonate most with you and watch what happens. Experiment. Play. Make it fun! You'll be proud of what your children are capable of.

We launched the Family Bank in our home when our three kids were five, seven, and nine. It changed our household dynamics for good. Here's our story with a blueprint for how you can implement it too.

---

[2] Driving the estate planning conversations with your aging parents is an entirely different conversation and out of scope of this book.

KIDS NEED TO UNDERSTAND MONEY

Personal Finance 101

Husband and I launched our children's financial journey four and a half years ago. At that time, none of the three understood what money is, where it comes from, and where it goes. They just knew they wanted control of it, and the sooner the better.

In our home, money is a finite resource that requires ongoing creative and thoughtful management. At the outset, our children didn't understand this.

They knew money is powerful, just as they intuitively understood that food, shelter, and (allegedly) video games are essential to life. The kids longed to engage with money on both the earning and burning sides of the equation. It's part of adulting, and what kid can't wait to grow up?

All three children routinely asked me why I had to leave home and go to work. At the beginning of 2019, 7-year-old Little Man held me up as I attempted to rush out the door.

> He beseeched me, "Why can't you stay with us? When are you going to retire?"
>
> "Little Man, I work so we can pay the bills. We must pay for our house, the electricity, and food."
>
> "But Mommy, your credit cards pay for that."

At that moment, it was clear that our children had major disconnects in their minds on how money works.

I made the decision to be a few minutes late to help him understand. On a small stool, I looked at him eye to eye.

> *"Yes Little Man, but we have to pay back the credit card companies."*
>
> *He paused. "Oh, you buy the credit cards then?"*
>
> *"Yes." (close enough) "That's the right concept. I go to work to buy the credit cards to pay for things."*
>
> *"Ohhhh, OK. I love you Mommy. Have a good day at the office."*

A year later, our three chickadees had dramatically advanced their understanding of money. The three years since then drove even more insights.

They learned how to make spending decisions, within the framework of their income and savings. They make tradeoffs between reusing materials on hand versus buying new. Sometimes they forgo small, immediate gratifications to save up for large purchases. They find ways to negotiate amongst themselves and partner together to get what they want sooner. The oldest started a neighborhood pet care business when she was nine; at thirteen she formed an LLC and opened a business bank account for it.

In short, they have more ownership of their financial future. The conversation no longer is "Mommy will you buy me ..." but rather "I have \$XYZ in my account, I'd like to buy ABC." The middle child is saving up his own money for a trip to Wrestlemania 2024 in Philadelphia.

By using a few simple principles and by sticking to them, your young household can go through an equally astonishing transformation.

This book shares both the philosophy and practical methods for teaching your kids how to harness their finances.

The punchline: Give them more control over the money you were already planning to spend on them.

The philosophy is about mindset and empowerment. Allow your children to make financial decisions. Help them experience the processes of earning, spending, and saving money. The better they become at making \$5, \$20, and \$100 decisions now, the better they'll be at \$50K, \$200K, and \$1MM decisions as adults. As with all skills, practice builds muscle memory.

> "Exposure from a young age to the realities of the world is a super-big thing."
> ~Bill Gates

Constrained Resources with an Abundance Mindset

Do you sometimes feel like Dr. No?
>Can I do this? No.
>Will you buy me that? No.
>I want this other thing! No.
>Can we go to Disneyworld? No.

Perhaps you have become a champion NOgotiator.

None of us enjoy being Mean Mom (or Dad) McMeanerson. I don't like saying "No" any more than they like hearing it. It adds negative energy to the home.

Children aren't born understanding the concept of constrained resources. They need to learn how to weigh two or more options and make informed decisions on how to use their money toward whatever desire they have. Without ample practice, how will your children gain the skills to make smart money decisions in the future?

Teach them how to manage their money and how to rebound from going broke while the stakes are low. It will reduce the likelihood of them going broke when it matters – and lower the probability of looking for you to bail them out at a higher cost. Despite the immediate distress this may cause, they will build confidence, resilience, and money management skills.

Constrained decision making is problem solving at its core. Foster a prosperity mindset. It's easy to fall into the classic "can't afford it" thinking. Identify what you can control. Look for solutions. Consider the different angles to get what you want. This is the mindset we want our children to embrace.

The easy ways to shut down spending discussions are rooted in a poor or scarcity mindset. Once we pivot the discussion to one of wealth and abundance, the discussion richens. Tap into your kids' natural creativity.

Poor Mindset	Prosperity Mindset
We can't afford it.	How *can* we afford this? Where can we cut back to make it work?
It's too expensive!	Is it worth it? Is the price negotiable? What are other options?
Money doesn't grow on trees.	How can we create extra income or make different choices?
We're not Jeff Bezos you know.	Let's look at how Jeff Bezos made his fortune and see what behaviors we can adopt too.
Do you think I'm made of money?	I'm not willing to spend my money on that. You are welcome to save up and spend yours.

Rather than focusing on not having enough, frame the conversation around how much it will take, and what needs to happen to get there. It may take some time to save up, with some other sacrifices along the way. Brainstorm how to bring the request to life instead of shutting it down.

By focusing everyone's energy on the solution, you are sending the signals that anything is possible if you work deliberately toward it. You must make tradeoffs to optimize spending where it matters most to you.

Initiate these discussions around dining out, going to the movies, having large vs. small birthday parties, buying the hundredth Pokémon™ card set, vacation planning, deciding which college to attend, and answering questions about why your car is a lot older than the Jones' next door. Involving the entire family in the decision-making process is vital for the kids' education.

The priorities we set and the priorities you set naturally will be different. Every family is unique. Make sure your family comes to a consensus on what it values to guide your discussions and financial decision making.

The kids may decide some sacrifices are not worth it. They may decide they are. That's the life skill to build. It boils down to what will bring you the most joy per dollar spent, one of my favorite money metrics.

Life is full of constrained resources that force choices. Choices are best made when priorities are carefully considered and agreed upon as a family. When we set out on this journey, it was time to expand our conversations. Our insight was to give our children control over more of the money we were spending on their behalf, and to teach them how to make their own financial decisions.

New Conversations

One of the unexpected benefits of giving the children more control over money was that it made our interactions smoother. After a couple of months, we started noticing easier exchanges.

> *Kid: "Mom, will you buy me a < >?"*
>
> *Mom: "I don't want to spend my money on it. It's not important to me. Would you like to spend your money?"*
>
> *Kid: "No."*
>
> *Mom: "OK."*

I told them I wouldn't spend my money, but they could spend theirs. That stopped many conversations in their tracks. I didn't have to tell them "No." It was easier than anticipated, and this repeated itself many times. Drop mic.

I make three points:

1. Parents do not have to be the bad guys, always saying "No." Habitual "Nos" provide constant fodder to rebel against and to resent.

   Helping each figure out how to afford what they want is fun. It shifts the conversation into a productive space and adds positivity to our relationship.

2. We actively discuss monetary value and family values. The value of the thing to me (zero), and what I am willing

to pay for it (zero), versus the value of the thing to them (greater than zero) and what they are willing to pay (debatable).

Rather than tell them how to make buying decisions, I show them how I do it when we're out shopping together. I consider the price and what it's worth to me. If price and value don't match, I don't spend my money. Each can make their own assessment.

3. This adds skin in the game, with their own tangible resources. If your kids are not willing to spend their hard-earned money, why should you?

    Skin in the game encourages thoughtful decision making and often better caretaking of the item (or greater appreciation of the experience) later.

We learn by observing others, followed by practicing new behaviors ourselves. With time and repetition, the behaviors grow into habits. Our kids will be making automatic tradeoff decisions based on what they observe us doing now, coupled with the muscle memory they build as they get ample opportunities to practice.

The Path to Abundance

Our goal is to teach Personal Finance to the next generation. It isn't rocket science:

- Buy less stuff.
- Spend less than you earn.
- If you want to spend more, earn more first.
- Have a bigger plan. Delay immediate gratification for more meaningful spending later.
- Put your savings dollars to work for you.
- Never forget the taxman. Don't waste energy letting taxes upset you because they're inevitable.[3]

I have no doubt that most readers of this book already have the financial knowledge. Here is a proven system for teaching these principles to your children in a hands-on, practical way. Our shared goal is that your kids learn how to make constrained resource decisions in an age-appropriate fashion. Give them more control at a very early age.

Through repeated practice, they will develop the behaviors and habits that will lead to abundance for the rest of their lives. Children who know how to manage their own finances grow into adults who confidently stand on their own two feet. With luck, they will also pass this onto your grandkids.

---

[3] Sure – you can employ some very sophisticated tax strategies, but that's not the first thing your children need to master as they enter the workforce.

A PLAN FOR THE NEXT GENERATION

A Heritage of Financial Literacy

Growing up, my sister and I had the benefit of parents with a deliberate approach to teaching good spending and saving habits. While formal jobs during the school year were discouraged, we babysat and did odd jobs to earn money on top of a modest allowance.

I'm dating myself, but in the 1980s, recycling was a new concept. It was common to see me collecting aluminum cans and newspapers from neighbors to haul to the recycling facility for cash, or selling tomato or strawberry plants to neighbors out of our little red wagon. My sister got a job at a local frozen yogurt shop one summer in high school, but most of the income was informal.

For every dollar earned, half went into the *"Brooks Bank"* to be saved. We surrendered the other half to our parents and recorded it on a paper spreadsheet. Our parents paid 1% monthly interest on the balances to encourage the savings habits. When either of us needed cash for spending, they gave us what we chose to withdraw. There was a catch though.

Before spending, we had to declare our intended purchase to a parent. Once declared, we had to wait two weeks before making the purchase. It created a cooling off period, designed to curb impulse spending.

It resulted in a few benefits:

1. Our parents always had an easy way to say no without actually saying no. Oh, how much we *hated* the cheerful, "Ok, wait two weeks!"

2. Regardless, either we totally forgot about whatever item it was that we could not live without,
    - or -
    We decided we didn't want to spend our money after all,
    - or -
    We bought stuff we actually wanted.

3. Impulse buying did not exist (with reasonable carry-over into adulthood purchasing patterns).

4. We built our executive functions, reinforcing the tremendous benefits of delaying gratification.

> Executive function is the set of cognitive processes that manage, control, and regulate other cognitive activities, including planning, working memory, attention, problem solving, impulse control, and flexible thinking.

The lessons these guardrails taught me have carried over well into adulthood. My sister and I are very mindful of money in different ways, resulting from how each of us internalized the pieces of our parents' personal finance lessons.

I am a natural saver now, and until the children came along, I excelled at living well beneath my means.

Husband's parents took a different approach. Both small business owners, the four children watched their parents immerse themselves in their companies. At times they too engaged in those family ventures. Today, one works in Corporate America, one is a public-school teacher, and two are professional real estate investors. All four are entrepreneurs with their own businesses: two part-time and two full-time.

His family focused less on teaching personal finance, where each child learned more by trial and error. Several of the kids held jobs in both high school and college, while tending to their studies.

Husband still shakes his head that his folks allowed him to buy a new car in high school. He took on debt at sixteen years old, necessitating a steady income. Since then, the only new vehicle he bought was the minivan we acquired twenty-one years later when our children entered the picture.

Through his experiences of early-onset debt, having to work from an early age, and being a small business owner himself, he developed frugality habits that serve him well. While readily picking up the tab for friends on a night out, or buying gifts he knows someone will love, he rarely spends on himself or makes large personal purchases. He's surprisingly minimalist.

Our plan for the next generation is to be deliberate in teaching personal finance early. The goal is to build upon what we individually learned from our childhood experiences and take it to the next level.

Money should entail both discipline and fun. It is neither good nor evil, but a device to be used however its wielder chooses.

"Money is only a tool. It will take you wherever you wish, but it will not replace you as the driver. It will give you the means for the satisfaction of your desires, but it will not provide you with desires."
~Ayn Rand, Atlas Shrugged

Formulating the Plan

To celebrate our tenth wedding anniversary, we left the kids with Grandma and slipped away to a historic inn in the picturesque Allegheny Mountains. We took advantage of the two-hour drive to develop our plan.

It was time to teach the littles how to earn money both actively and passively. We wanted the children to learn about taxes and savings the hard way, by forcing the haircut off gross earnings. They would experience how their choices make the balances go up - and go down. They would learn empirically, seeing how their actions and decisions had natural consequences, for better and for worse.

We were excited to see how it would play out. Each child has a very different personality, and each would care more about certain aspects than others. We were curious how quickly each would figure out how to game the system, placing our bets on who would be the spender(s) and who would be the saver(s).

Now we needed to solidify the details of the plan and open the doors of our new bank for business. Step one was to create the opening balance for each account based on cash in hand.

Confiscating Cash

The Lennon children formally adopted a cashless economy on the evening of January 20, 2019. Husband commenced the ceremonies by sending them off to round up the money in their possession. They purged their rooms of all US currency and met back at the kitchen table, returning with denominations ranging from pennies and golden dollars to two-dollar bills and Andrew Jacksons.

We made it clear that there was to be no more cash in anyone's rooms. We encouraged each child to do one final check, and to think through where else money might be hiding. Any cash that surfaced  thereafter became Mom & Dad's without debate.

Little Man started to panic. Grandma had given them each small bags of coins at the holidays, and he didn't know where his pouch was. He estimated it had $7.50 in it. We gave him the benefit of the doubt and added that sum to his total with the expectation that once it turned up, he'd hand it over.

Upon dumping their piles of loot, they lined up the coins in stacks of ten. I found coin wrappers and the family started rolling up by denomination. Each child did the math to count his or her riches.

The girls announced that they had combined their resources a while back, which sounded good until Baby Girl objected to splitting it in half. That launched a brief and decisive discussion about what it means to combine finances, and a strong recommendation not to do that again anytime soon. She resigned herself to the 50/50 split that Husband mandated.

They inquired about the Amazon gift cards they'd received. We added the balances to their spending ledgers, while they physically surrendered the cards to me. After a moment of panic, the kids were reassured that if they wanted to use their money at Amazon, they could (with my help), with or without gift cards in hand.

With holiday gift cards and Grandma's magic pouch taken into consideration, plus an extra little padding for the younger two, each child had the following starting balances in their spending accounts:

> Baby Girl (Age 9½): $57.25
>
> Little Man (Age 7½): $45.00
>
> Wee One (Age 5½): $45.00

Everyone agreed that there were no outstanding IOUs.

As we cleared the cash and gift cards from the table, the older two looked bewildered. Tears welled up. Little Man thought he was losing his dough. Baby Girl was uncertain, while Wee One had no idea what was really happening. Husband and I paused, realizing we had not adequately explained how the electronic economy would work.

It took a few different approaches, helping them understand that this would be very good for each of them. We had to show how even if the physical currency was not theirs to keep in their rooms, their purchasing power remained.

Transparent Accounting

The family needed an initial system to account for the money. I created a simple Google Sheets ledger in my account, sharing it with a family account where the children could access it on their own in read-only mode. They could see where their accounts stood at any time. We didn't need a fancy tool; simply two ledgers per child: one for spending and one for saving.

In Google Sheets, this translated to a very simple table, duplicated three times (one per child). Each entry would be dated, with the starting balance, transaction amount, and updated balance like in a checkbook register.

I added a final column to record the transaction's purpose, anticipating future disputes, and skepticism over where all the money had gone. Every adult on earth has asked that question at least once. It was fair to expect the children would have those same moments of disbelief.

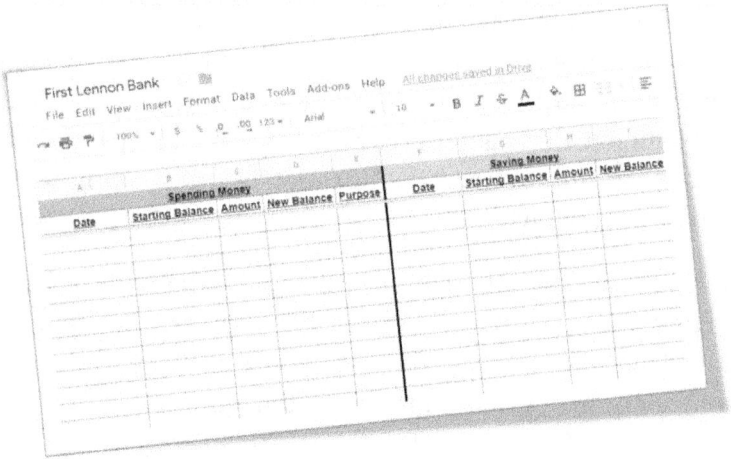

To illustrate how the ledger works, Husband put each child's total in their spending column, showing them that they had credit for every dollar they previously had. He explained how each child still had that much money to use and that we would hand it over when they wished to spend it. The only difference was that the family would track it on the spreadsheet where anyone could see their balances any time they wanted.

To engage the young clientele in this new financial institution, they were invited to name it, thus instilling a sense of ownership in their personal financial institution. After vetoing any potty words, the crew christened their new treasury the *First Lennon Bank*.

If you want this simple ledger for your family, go to www.magnifiyourlife.com/resources to take a free copy.

Household Contributions

Once we knew how we were going to track the money, we set up ways for the kids to earn money. It started with chores.

Chores and family responsibilities are critical for several reasons. Selfishly, they make parents' lives easier when the children help out. This is the least of the benefits however, when trying to raise productive members of society.

Research shows that children who have family and household responsibilities develop stronger executive skills, higher self-esteem, and greater senses of responsibility. They get the satisfaction that accompanies (1) the sense of accomplishment, and (2) belonging to something greater than themselves.

While no seven year old will articulate this of their own accord, you are planting seeds that are more stubborn than any weed on earth. They will germinate within and serve your children well.

It is important that kids view themselves as important parts of the family, and that what they do matters. Feeling connected to others has been proven to bolster self-esteem, self-worth, and self-control. These matter when the child is trying to decide how to handle peer pressure. Do they give in to their peer group, or stay true to the values that their family unit has laid down? The stronger the sense of family, connection, and shared values is, the higher the likelihood that they will make choices aligned with the family's values.

On top of feelings of worth and value, performing acts of service to the family gives each child confidence and life skills. We won't be there forever to spot Baby Girl a $20, pick up after Little Man, or wash Wee One's clothes. Nor should we be.

They need to know how to handle their own hygiene, manage their living space, properly feed themselves, look after other living creatures (pet, houseplant, or other family members), and know how to contribute to a household in general. The more they practice, the more these activities become non-events. Children grow into young adults who are fully capable of taking care of themselves.

The more they can manage their day to day lives AND their finances, the less likely they will boomerang home later in life. While being compassionate if a child needs a helping hand from time to time, we want that to be a low probability, temporary exception, not a norm.

If you have ever had an awful roommate or if your spouse never learned how to get along without Mama, you know what I am getting at. It can even show up in workplace behaviors. Don't let your kids become that annoying roommate, spouse, or coworker. Chores should be age-appropriate in quantity, complexity, and standards of execution. See the Resources section on page 97 for several ideas.

On their first several attempts, you will need to be more involved, modeling the activity and helping the little ones learn how to do the work. After several at-bats at each activity, the child should be given the opportunity to do their tasks solo.

While perfection is unfair to expect out of the gates, make sure that you uphold a certain standard of "done." If you go back afterwards to finish a task, you are telling your child that it's ok to be sloppy about their work. What they do doesn't actually matter, and someone else will fix it anyway. Quality is someone else's job. They aren't good enough. These are terrible messages to send to your children.

When you can make chores fun, do it. If the kids want to draw pictures in the dust or pollen before wiping it away, let them. If they enjoy vacuuming patterns in the carpet, as long as they cover the whole floor space, so what? Maybe there is a bonus for chores done by a certain early deadline. The goal is to get the work done while teaching life skills and making your child stronger. It's not to make everyone routinely miserable.

Active Income

If you can work it into your household finances, give your children the opportunity to earn an allowance. Ours had been asking how they could earn money and were primed for the discussion. They were not in a hurry to do more work around the house but realized that was one way to coax the almighty dollar out of us.

Whereas the family had attempted to start an allowance before, it was abandoned after a week or two. With ages spanning five to nine at the beginning, we agreed it was time to offer allowance, while laying down more explicit expectations for the children to engage in the household. This was overdue.

Bluntly, the children were not pulling their age-appropriate weight within the family. They weren't learning the value of hard work, the feeling of satisfaction upon earning fair compensation, or the basic skills to get along later in life without their significant others or roommates evicting them.

Equally importantly, we needed help. With multiple full-time jobs and side hustles, we had to get ourselves ready at the beginning of the day too. Getting up earlier to take care of kid basics was getting old. Offering an allowance as incentive to pick up more responsibilities at home solved multiple problems, while mirroring the "real world" of going to work and getting paid for it.

Chores and allowance deliberately did not come with an à la carte option, where someone could forgo a portion to avoid an undesirable task. While doing chores and receiving allowance were tied together, opting out of chores on an ongoing basis was not an option. Responsibilities were expected as an integral part of being in the family. We provided allowances to offer the children opportunities to buy goods and services that were important to them.

On a positive note, each child *wanted* opportunities to earn more spending money. The kids had already tasted entrepreneurship, setting up neighborhood lemonade stands and participating in the community yard sale. They wanted more.

Clearly, we had to offer alternate paths to practice the art of spending - *and not spending* - money.

All Hail the Taxman

In the real world, most earnings are subject to income tax of some variety. The taxman comes knocking like clockwork. An entire industry is built around helping people and legal entities minimize their tax burden.

For most of us, taxes are an unavoidable reality for much of our lives. The gross you earn is only yours to keep if you earn it in a tax-free vehicle. While possible to play deep tax games (legally), most of us need to resign ourselves to and plan for taxes, at least at the beginning of our earning lifecycle.

Although they are quite young, it seemed wise to help the littles get used to it now. To that end, we established a 50% tax rate. Yes, you read that right. 50%.

It is easy to calculate, and once used to it, anything lower is a blessing. It helps accustom them to the real income they earn, and to living within their means. This worked well at the **Brooks Bank** and was adopted by the **First Lennon Bank**.

Taxing the children's income in this way serves multiple purposes. The first lesson it provides is that the amount your employer pays you is NOT equivalent to your purchasing power. Almost all US income is subject to income tax, with a few notable exceptions that will not be covered in this book.

Our logic is that the sooner each realizes their paychecks get automatic haircuts, the more they'll frame their thinking around it appropriately. They can't fight the IRS; it's best to find a way to deal amicably with it.

The Secret to Taxes: If you know you want X of net, negotiate X+Y of gross to cover the government's share. The total was never fully yours to begin with.

Since I grew up with access to only half my income, it helped me look at taxes in a somewhat neutral light, while teaching me to live below my net income, vs. my gross.

In reality, this 50% is not going to the IRS. Look at it as forced savings. In the children's case, the mandatory 50% haircut is going into an interest-bearing savings account or brokerage account. It is tracked alongside the spending ledger and will be held in custody until they graduate high school and are off to college or whatever follows graduation for each.

Regardless of the IRS or a savings account simulating the income tax, the goal is to encourage a high savings rate, while illustrating the power of compound interest and passive income generation.

Savings and Passive Income

As a member of the **Brooks Bank** growing up, my sister and I had to sock away half of everything we earned. This practice offered delayed benefits. I had what felt like a small fortune (~$2000[4]) going into college. It more than covered my pocket money needs for a few years.

Not being a huge spender, I made it last. I only lightly augmented it throughout the school year, plus summer job income. We plan to pass on this same gift to our three when they are ready for their next adventure, college or otherwise. These spending accounts will contribute to their own pocket money as well as room and board when they fly the nest.

Littles are never too young to learn about saving, investing, and the beauty of compound interest. The **First Lennon Bank** pays dividends ("bonuses" in kid speak) for balances carried to the first day of each month.

Albert Einstein is rumored to have remarked, "The most powerful force in the universe is compound interest."

---

[4] Worth ~$4,600 in 2023 dollars after 33 years plus post-pandemic inflation

Being more of a physicist than an economist, I don't know if he actually said it, and I never had the chance to ask him directly. If he didn't, I'm more than happy to take credit for this deep thought.

After surrendering their currency, each child received a starter "savings account" of $30.00. This piqued their interest and the tears dried up. Husband explained how the *First Lennon Bank* calculates and pays bonuses on the first of each month on both the savings and spending accounts.

Although interest rates on savings accounts haven't been this high since when we were kids[5], we set the household interest rate at 12% annually. While this will not be matched at a public bank anytime soon, it is easy for kids to calculate.

Husband showed them a quick tutorial about how they earn 1% each month. They can look at their balance and move the decimal over by two places. It's both a teachable math moment and an easy calculation.

Given the order of magnitude on the dollars in question, it started out as peanuts on an absolute scale. We can afford it. If a different interest rate works for you, go for it. I do recommend that you model out whatever you land on though, so YOU are not caught off-guard later yourself by the power of compound interest. [6]

---

[5] The all-time high for the prime rate was 21.50% in 1980.

[6] Having modeled this out with simple compounding math, we anticipate each child will have saved a minimum of $10,000 in their savings accounts by the time they graduate high school. Interestingly, assuming the allowance holds steady

Initially, each account earned very little because the balances were small. However, since they could only deplete their spending account, they observed how their savings earned increasing dividend payments as the balances increased.

After month 1, their $30.00 savings generated $0.30. After month 2, they each had received four $10.00 allowance payments (more on this to come). Their $70.30 savings generated $0.70. Between the balance and the dividend increases, over time they will see how larger balances earn larger dividends.

> "Do not save what is left after spending,
> but spend what is left after saving."
> ~Warren Buffett

There are several lessons here. The simplest one is, "The more money your account holds, the bigger the bonus." This took a few months to register as they saw what happened based on the balances they carried, while peeking at what their siblings got. We heard, "No Fair!!" for the first two or three months. On the contrary, nothing could be fairer. Each has an equal opportunity to earn, spend, and save. Natural consequences are a powerful instructor.

Secondly is the lesson of compound interest. It is unnoticeable at the small dollar amounts, and went ignored in the spending

---

throughout their adolescence (may or may not be a fair assumption), their monthly passive income from interest will exceed earned income [from allowance] approximately 5.5 years into this grand experiment, shortly before the oldest turns 15.

accounts for a while. However, the savings accounts are untouchable. The interest has built up considerably.

The third lesson feeds off the first two, which is the power of passive income. Showing the children how their money can work for them is incredibly persuasive. The earlier they internalize this, even if in a fuzzy notion at first, the better off their entire financial future may be.

Spending With Purpose and Within Boundaries

Cash burns holes in children's pockets. Once they have some, they want to spend it immediately. This can often manifest as wandering aimlessly around Target or the Dollar Store searching for something to buy.

The ideal purchasing pattern is to decide what you plan to buy in advance, make sure you have sufficient funds to cover the purchase without sacrificing other life essentials, and make the purchase without adding other unplanned items to your shopping cart. Marketers everywhere will try to overcome your resolve. The goal is to stay focused on the prize, and make it back home with any excess funds still in our bank account or pocket.

One anticipated challenge was tackling spending money at actual stores for toys, and encouraging them to think of other ways to enjoy their hard-earned money. Little Man is a big sports kid. He always begged to go to the driving range, glow-golf, bowling, Sky Zone, Chuck E Cheese, etc. This presented the opportunity to expand his thinking on what he could save and spend his money on. Before rushing off to Target or the Dollar Store with fists of cash, we encouraged him to consider alternate ways for his spending money to create joy for himself and possibly others.

Secondly, we learned that it is important to establish upfront boundaries of what the kids are allowed to spend their money on. Are you ok with them buying sweets or fast food, and does that mean they can eat however much, whenever they want to? Are you ok with them buying electronics? If so, are there time or other usage limitations that apply? Is there a limit to how much online gaming they can fund? If they buy their own clothes, are there length, coverage, or other restrictions that apply (e.g., no holes, or no profanity/objectionable graphics)?

It's important to share that we also expected and HOPED one or more would go hog wild with their spending accounts and go broke once or more along the journey (Little Man obliged us). It's ideal for it to happen in elementary school, with hopes that they learn how to course-correct and spend wisely as early as possible. If this never happens before college, it is a lost opportunity for safe learning.

Structured failure is one of the best gifts parents can orchestrate. Make sure they internalize the right lessons from it.

"Don't tell me where your priorities are. Show me where you spend your money and I'll tell you what they are."
~ James W. Frick

Game On!

At the end of the discussion, all five family members were excited to see where it went. Without being fully aware of it, the children were to become our juvenile personal finance guinea pigs. We were curious what would work, and what would blow up in our faces with unintended consequences.

The next step: formalizing chores and an allowance.

THE GRAND EXPERIMENT

Putting the Kids to Work

The next step was identifying household responsibilities for each child. We decided the chickadees could be responsible for getting themselves ready for each school day. If they chose to dilly dally and go without breakfast or making their lunch, it would be self-correcting as the child went hungry or spent their own money on school provisions. Neither would kill them while offering first-hand life lessons.

The kids started brainstorming other chore ideas. We slid in a few others. Some were expected throughout the week, such as feeding the pets daily or emptying the dishwasher on an as-needed basis. Other weekly activities could be done at the children's time discretion, but no later than mid-day Sunday.

Beyond the morning flurry, several other tasks fell squarely into kid skillsets. They had already started setting the dinner table, accompanied by the privilege of deciding who got to sit next to whom. Clearing the table was much less enticing, but they engaged when asked.

The desired new behavior was to go beyond stacking dishes on the counter or in the sink and ensure they made it into the dishwasher. Starting the dishwasher became a favorite job that each initially enjoyed. Once clean, the older two could empty the whole dishwasher, using chairs to reach the cupboards, and the youngest could put away the silverware. As the littlest got older, she joined the rotation for fully emptying the dishwasher on her own.

Initially, they were asked to tidy their rooms before bed roughly every other evening, including getting dirty laundry into the baskets *turned the right side out*. They carried these baskets downstairs on laundry day, and helped get the machine loaded and started. Once a week they vacuumed their rooms, as a prerequisite to collecting their weekly allowance payment. As they got older, they took on full responsibility for their own laundry, including folding and putting it away.

The final expectation was that they would each engage more actively in taking care of the dog. When Mr. Toad joined the family six months earlier, each swore up and down that he or she would take care of him at every turn. Not surprisingly, this tapered off quickly. The kids cheerfully gave him his meals, but they had to be reminded constantly.

Before installing the fence, Mr. Toad enjoyed long walks 2-3 times each day. After the fence gave him free rein of the yard and the weather started getting colder, walks became sporadic. The kids rotated whose turn it was to pick up the poop while walking, but when left to his own devices in the yard, Mr. Toad left landmines everywhere. Nobody put effort into cleaning up after him.

Since they were getting new responsibilities, the final task preceding payday was for each to pick up five poop piles and deposit them in the waste bin. In advance of payday seemed to be the moment they would be most motivated to hop to it.

One week the youngest decided she wasn't going to do her weekend chores. She was asked and reminded several times. Ultimately, she received no weekly allowance.

It was pointed out later when the children were reviewing their ledger updates, to make sure the consequences of non-participation were not lost on any of them. If it were to become a pattern, the consequences would become more impactful, but after four years there have been only two cases where a child refused to do their household duties and forfeited their weekly stipend.

An Eternal School Lunch Debate: Bring or Buy

School lunches were both the initial test and the basis for setting their initial allowance amount.

They LOVE buying lunch at school, both because they like many of the food options and because it was an uncommon event. We started elementary school with the intention of ensuring they have healthy options packed with love each day. It lasted for three and a half school years, and quite frankly, we got tired. Worse yet, the kids didn't appreciate it.

Buy Days were usually a result of me running late and not having the time to make lunch or Husband being in charge and giving them the nod. Upon further reflection, we had made their own lunches as long as they could remember.

Why not the chickadees? Check. One more task to kidsource.

The new deal: make their own lunch from home, using whatever was in the house, or buy their lunch with the $2.40 per meal coming from their spending money.

With this in mind, we set their weekly allowance at $20. Half would go straight to savings. If they chose to buy their lunch, they could buy up to four days a week.

We stocked the fridge with many options for easily assembling their lunches if they wanted. They held the control in their own hands over spending on school lunches or pocketing the cash.

When they heard this, six bright blue eyes lit up.

We knew full well that for at least the first few weeks, each child would put their own budget to the test on school lunches alone. It was a powerful teaching moment, and one that would teach itself. We were right.

Two days after our kickoff, the children decided to buy their lunches that week using the funds they already had. This was a big deal because buying school lunch had been a rare treat. It was a short holiday week, and the girls bought all four days. The boy bought three days.

When Husband and I were kids, lunch was cash based. You brought your $1.10, selected your pizza slice or cheeseburger, grabbed the hottest fries available, chose between skim, whole, and chocolate milk, and paid the cashier at the end of the lunch counter.

Lunch transactions happen a bit differently today. The kids have plastic cards which get funded behind the scenes. Students make their lunch selections and hand their card to the cashier. Money is disassociated from the purchase of food, not unlike any other transaction in life with the prevalence of debit and credit cards. It does, however, bypass the education of where the value originates. It also gives parents full visibility into what the students purchase and presumably eat.

The children felt liberated with their new spending power. They bought extra chips and dessert. It was a free for all. I peeked at their tabs partway through the week and gave them grief about the extras they were buying. I knew full well they were throwing away fruits and vegetables in lieu of the junk.

Noticing the girls bought cupcakes, I commented on the price. Baby Girl was horrified, not realizing they were costing her $0.85 each.

At the end of the first week, Little Man was the only one who didn't lose money at the cafeteria. Both girls exceeded their $10 income with $11.55 (WO) and $11.60 (BG). These amounts came off the ledgers on Sunday. It sobered them to see how quickly the money evaporated.

Midway through week two, each looked at it differently, though all agreed that buying lunch was awesome.

9-year-old Baby Girl (BG):

Mom: "Tell me about buying lunch."

Baby Girl: "School lunches usually cost $2.40, and that's kind of a lot of money. You only get $20 a week. You get to spend $10 and save $10."

Mom: "How much did you spend this week?"

BG: "At lunch this week, so far I've only spent $2.40. My goal is to spend about $4.80 a week."

Mom: "What's the best part about buying lunch?"

BG: "I love the food there. That's why I buy. But I know I'll use all my money if I buy every day. I plan to buy on Wednesday and Friday. Every other Wednesday you get French Toast sticks - I love 'em! Friday you get Pizza!!"

7-year-old Little Man (LM):

Mom: "Who paid for your lunches last week?"

Little Man: "Me!!!"

Mom: "How did that feel?"

LM: "Good. The girls spent $6 more than me."

Mom: "So what did that mean at the end of the week? That you spent less money than them?"

LM: "I get $4.10."

> Mom: *"Where did that $4.10 go?"*
>
> LM: *"My spending account where I can buy stuff."*
>
> Mom: *"What will you do differently this week?"*
>
> LM: *"I'm not spending so I can have more money."*
>
> Mom: *"What are you going to do with that money?"*
>
> LM: *"Buy a phone or something."*

5-year-old Wee One (WO):

> Mom: *"What did you spend at lunch this week?"*
>
> Wee One: *"Ummmm, $2.25?"*
>
> Mom: *"No, $11.00. What did you earn this week?"*
>
> WO: *"$10.00"*
>
> Mom: *"You spent more than you earned. What happens if you spend more than you earn all the time?"*
>
> WO: *[SHRUG]*
>
> Mom: *"You run out of money. If you have zero dollars, what do you get to buy at Target?"*
>
> WO: *"Nothing!"*
>
> Mom: *"Do you want to buy nothing at Target?"*
>
> WO: *"No!"*
>
> Mom: *"What will you do differently this week?"*

> WO: *"Pack my lunch!"*
>
> Mom: *"Did you buy or bring today?"*
>
> WO: *"Bring!"*
>
> Mom: *"Did that save you money?"*
>
> WO: *"Yes!!"*
>
> Mom: *"Cool! What are you going to do tomorrow?"*
>
> WO: *"Bring!"*

After a week and a half, things were looking promising on the school lunch front. Each kid started connecting the dots between what they do and how it translates to spending power.

Baby Girl identified where it was worth spending her money, specifically on French Toast sticks. Little Man identified a path to saving money toward larger purchases. Wee One was still a bit clueless, but she made a couple lunches the second week anyway.

Putting a bow on top - neither parent spent our time assembling lunches. The kids were responsible and gained a new element of control over their daily lives.

First Payday!!

At the end of week one, the kids were anxious to get paid and go shopping.

Before any money moved through the *First Lennon Bank*, this was our opportunity to get some chores done while teaching responsibility. The children had been doing some work to help the family throughout the week, and there was more to do. We started out strong.

- ☐ Clean rooms (x3)
- ☐ Vacuum rooms (x3)
- ☐ Empty dishwasher (LM)
- ☐ Empty trash bins and replace bin liners (BG)
- ☐ Right-side out laundry and start a load (LM)
- ☐ Pick up dog poop from the yard (10 per person, since we'd been lax for a while).

There was a flurry of excitement and anticipation, blended with the occasional argument (who got to vacuum first), punctuated with the unexpected collaboration and kindness as Little Man helped Baby Girl carry the vacuum down the stairs. After the last pile of poo was scooped, and all six hands were thoroughly washed, it was time to move money.

Each child excitedly saw their weekly allowance added to their ledgers - $10 on the left, and $10 on the right.

The dismay started when they had to witness the effects of their cafeteria spending. Little Man was a bit ahead of last week, but the sweets and Cheez-Its set the girls back. There were a few "Awwws" but as each had a positive starting point, nobody felt any pain yet. It fostered good conversations, including the opportunity to influence the grocery list.

Next was the opportunity to spend their allowance. The kids had been looking forward to this all week. We tried several approaches to slow them down, including offering a $5 bonus for spending nothing, and a $2 bonus for spending the least of the three.

We attempted to pin them down on exactly what they wanted to avoid wandering the aisles of Target aimlessly. Only Wee One could crisply articulate exactly what she wanted and where it was in the store.

It was looking like everyone wanted more Pokémon™ cards and stuff, despite our house being littered with hundreds of these little collectable cards. Husband tried every argument on earth to offer different ideas.

> *"Why are you buying more of what you already have? How about something new?"*

"Do you guys even play the game?"

"How about saving your money for the Nintendo™ Switch you were eyeing?"

The kids were determined.

We headed to the store as a family. Husband set a 10 minute deadline to make their selections and get to the checkout line. Wee One found her coveted item in 12 seconds. Baby Girl and Little Man took the full amount of time. We walked out of the store with $70 of Pokémon™ stuff (augmenting their allowance with pre-existing funds from their ledgers), and the children were elated.

Baby Girl got the $2 bonus, spending $0.60 less than her younger siblings. All three went to bed happy.

Change in the Sofa

Throughout the first couple of weeks additional cash surfaced. Each was diligent in bringing it to our attention as soon as it was located, ranging from two pennies to a tray of small change. The children's disappointment was evident, with each coin they turned in.

The children also found random coins while out and about. The oldest spotted a quarter and a penny in a store parking lot, which she turned in to be added to her ledger. Every found penny was given due respect, and it showed up as a line item. The lesson: even pennies should be minded.

While that lesson may or may not sink in solely through these practices, it created an opportunity for me to share my triumphs as a kid in being the best coin spotter in the family.

When I was their age, we had coin operated public phones and soda machines. Dollar and credit card devices hadn't yet been added. My finger went into every coin return I passed. It became a running family joke. The best I did was find a $20 bill on a store floor. I collected over $100 from other people's negligence by the time I'd graduated college. I'm proud of that.

As a side note, Little Man (now 12) figured out on his own that vending machines are a source of treasure. Imagine my surprise (and secret thrill) when I saw him find a few quarters in a coin return not too long ago. I didn't know they took coins anymore. Now he won't go past a vending machine without checking. Though it slows us down, it makes me smile.

First of the Month Dividends

February 1, 2019 was our first opportunity to pay and discuss dividends, interest, or bonus payouts. Use the terminology that resonates most with your children. Ours understood the concept of "bonuses" so we went with that.

First, we had to help them understand the difference between active and passive income. I recorded the following conversation with Baby Girl in early February.

Mom: *"Let me tell you what passive means and what active means. Active is like activity, where you do stuff. Like chores, you must do something to earn money. What's another example of active income?"*

BG: *"Hot cocoa stand!"*

Mom: *"Right! How does Mommy earn money?"*

BG: *"Go to work!"*

Mom: *"If I stop going, what happens to the money?"*

BG: *"Bye Bye"*

Mom: *"The money stops. Wouldn't it be great to earn money without having to do any work?"*

BG: *"Yay!!"*

Mom: *"That's called Passive Income. Have you ever heard of money making money for you?"*

BG: *"No."*

Mom: *"But wait! Didn't you just get a bonus?"*

BG: *"Yeah! 27¢ because I saved $27.00."*

Mom: *"What if you had $37.00 or only $17.00?"*

BG: *"I'd get more or I'd get less!"*

Mom: *"The more you save, the harder your money works for you. If Mommy's money works hard enough for her… does Mommy still have to work?"*

BG: *"No. We could go out more, and we could have lunch together more, and you can be mystery reader more, and you could do a lot of things more instead of working in a boring office."*

After several months, preliminary results were in. There wasn't enough data to show a significant trend, but it started conversations about the benefits of delaying or not spending.

First Year Dividend Payouts

Month	9-10 yr old		7-8 yr old		5-6 yr old	
	Spend	Save	Spend	Save	Spend	Save
January	$0.27	$0.42	$0.39	$0.40	$0.13	$0.40
February	$0.33	$0.82	$0.60	$0.80	$0.07	$0.70[7]
March	$0.61	$1.23	$0.57	$1.31	$0.19	$1.21
April	$1.35	$2.14	$0.57	$1.73	$0.47	$1.62
May	$1.50	$2.57	$0.43	$2.14	$0.49	$2.04
June	$029	$3.17	$1.44	$2.69	$0.82	$2.56
July	$0.62	$3.65	$1.40	$3.12	$1.22	$2.99
August	$1.60	$4.24	$1.90	$3.70	$2.18	$3.57
September	$0.27	$4.72	$0.31	$4.13	$0.98	$4.04
October	$0.83	$5.41	$0.26	$4.60	$0.98	$4.48
November	$0.00	$5.94	$0.18	$5.00[8]	$0.19	$4.98
December	$1.21	$7.15	$0.04	$5.45	$0.58	$5.43

---

[7] One week the youngest flat out refused to do her chores, and she saw the consequences with no allowance.

[8] Another week, Little Man made the conscious choice to forgo payday in lieu of chores after an exhausting camping weekend.

While the younger two each lost their allowance once (thus losing revenue), Baby Girl started a neighborhood pet sitting business, which boosted both her spending and savings.

Otherwise, the differences were predominantly tied to spending (or lack thereof). Each child used some of their spending money for holiday gifts for one another, some being more generous than others.

As each month passes, they witness the difference between the savings and spending accounts. Interest gained on the savings account is close to what the spending account interest would have been, had they chosen not to spend their money.

As it compounds and they continue to spend, this amount has become noticeably different. After a few months, it was not even a dollar. While a dollar still is significant at this age, the gap will become painful as that difference widens.

The spending accounts fluctuate dramatically, but the savings continue to grow steadily. Four years into this, the monthly savings interest ranges from $26 to $37 per month, depending on the child's accrued savings. It is becoming meaningful.

Creating New Revenue

"World's Best Lemonade" Stand

Over the summer of 2019[9], the girls decided to host a lemonade, cookie, and candy stand at the neighborhood pool. At

---

[9] Sadly the Pandemic put a hold on lemonade stands for the next two years

first, I bought all the supplies (the most profitable), or some of the supplies (moderately profitable). To educate them on how business really works, now they must cover their variable supplies. The girls were up for the challenge.

We bought lemons and sugar, boxes of Starburst and Skittles, and materials for my best chocolate chip cookie recipe. We calculated how much ingredients cost, and by extension the cost of goods for the cookies, lemonade, and candy.

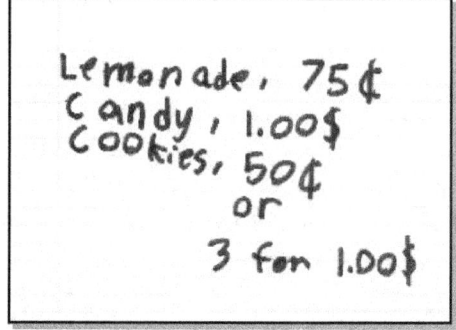

Lemonade, 75¢
Candy, 1.00$
Cookies, 50¢
or
3 for 1.00$

With that, the girls baked cookies and squeezed lemons. They set their prices to ensure they had a chance to be profitable. We discussed volume pricing for the cookies and they landed on 50¢ each, or 3 for $1.

After hauling our goods to the pool, they had to balance engaging customers with not eating their inventory.

We discussed our customer targeting, based on what we observed. Teenagers were most likely to buy the candy. Dads and older neighbors were more likely to be drawn to the lemonade. The cookies tempted everyone and who could blame them? They were still soft from the oven and smelled great.

Baby Girl is a raging introvert. She had to put herself out there, calling out to neighbors hawking the "best lemonade in

Virginia," "fresh baked chocolate chip cookies" and "candy!" depending on the demographic of the passer-by. One neighbor overpaid and asked us to give his "credits" to his grandkids who stopped by later. The girls practiced making change and saying thank you.

Between selling the world's best lemonade and having extremely generous neighbors, they were able to earn a bit of spending money after each effort.

They practiced:

- Sourcing (buying the raw materials)

- Production (squeezing lemons and mixing the juice with water and sugar)

- Marketing (colorful signs and loudly announcing their product to passersby)

- Fulfillment (serving the lemonade)

- Customer Service (collecting payment, making change, and thanking their customers)

- Logistics (set-up and breakdown of their stand)

- Accounting (counting their revenues, and reimbursing me for the upfront investment)

While they grumbled lightly at the cost of goods that came out of their revenues, they started getting the concepts. Light bulbs went off in the children's minds. They realized that cash is fun, and that they can earn it - enabling them to spend more.

At the end, as the food truck nearby closed up shop, we started putting away our leftovers. The food truck staff brought over a tray of funnel cake fries, and we returned the favor with cookies. Everyone was happy, while also being ready to be done for the afternoon.

After they counted their revenues and netted off the costs, the girls each had $7.95 to show for their efforts. Half went into their savings, for a net of $3.98 each. Not much to show for many hours of work, but profitable and they had fun. On a relative basis, it boosted their weekly income by 40%; that $4 meant something.

Pet Sitting

Baby Girl loves animals and is the ultimate dog lover. When a neighbor asked her to look after their dog and plants for a week, she beamed with excitement. To have the opportunity to earn money doing what she loves is the dream that most people harbor.

She showed up with her notebook and pushed her shy self to speak to the neighbor, asking questions and taking detailed notes. She collected the necessary instructions, and carefully took custody of the key.

The first pup gave her a run for her money. She patiently coaxed him to let her pet him after taking care of business outside and eating. To be paid for the privilege of playing with him and being entrusted with the responsibility was icing on the cake.

As is customary, half went into the savings account, and half went into the spending account on payday.

After her first engagement, she happily took on more work. A second neighbor invited her to look after two dogs and a cat, and her business began. Having seen Husband's and my examples, she asked to print business cards to share with more neighbors. We found a design online that she liked, and she used her spending money to order 500. That gave her enough to put in mailboxes, reserving some to hand out when she showed up at engagements.

After receiving the precious box of cards in the mail, Baby Girl and Little Man rode their bikes to put one in each nearby neighbor's mailbox. Other days we walked.

As we encountered neighbors, I nudged Baby Girl to open the conversation and tell them about her business. There is a big difference between handing someone a card and talking about your services eye to eye, versus anonymously leaving a business card to be thrown out with the other random junk that shows up in a mailbox.

A few days later, her second customer posted a picture of her card on our active neighborhood Facebook group with a recommendation. The following day, an email inquiry came in from a new customer who needed her two cats fed during the holidays. And thus a multi-year income stream began.

Yardwork for Hire

In early August, the family took a trip to Nana's mountain house. As a master naturalist for the Wintergreen Foundation, the intrusion of stilt grass angered Nana. It was taking over the mountain's natural vegetation.

Nana offered the children the opportunity to earn a few dollars helping her remove this unwanted invasion from her yard. The four of them spent about thirty minutes pulling the offensive grass out, earning $10 each for their efforts, knowing that half was to go into their spending, and half into savings. Little Man decided he wanted it all to go into his savings, even though he

knew that once it went into the saving account, it could not come back.

The children don't normally engage in a lot of manual labor, and seldom choose to help me out in the garden when I ask. My interview results were amusing.

> *Baby Girl: "It was hard work, because, you had to pick a thousand million weeds. But because they came loose easily from the ground, the thirty minutes really only felt like five."*

> *Little Man: "The work was really easy. It was hard to work around the other plants, and I got pricklied through the back of my gloves. It kind of hurt, but Papa pulled the prickers out. I'd do it again if Nana wanted to hire me again. When I saw all the bags of grass, I was really proud of myself."*

> *Wee One: "It was OK. I mean I loved it! It was really great because I got money. I thanked Nana because she gave us the choice for picking weeds." [Hears an intriguing noise from downstairs] "I'm going downstairs. You finish the rest of your book."*

There are many creative ways to help family and neighbors with maintaining their yards. The boy across the street mows lawns. Another neighbor posted an online request for a teenager who could dig a hole for her. One year our kids sold their services picking up acorns from yards, which they later fed to the pigs up the road. The ideas are endless.

We want the kids to see financial opportunity everywhere. The most interesting side hustles I see are born out of creativity (and sometimes boredom). Yards and gardens have a ton of opportunity for creative income generation without needing a lot of skillsets or startup capital.

Educational Incentives

Education is extremely important to us. To encourage reading when it was an unpopular activity, we put a monetary incentive on reading accomplishments.

The carrot was this: $50 to each child who reads 100 chapter books.[10] Note that this is not 50¢ per book; it's all or nothing. They had to read the book, provide a verbal synopsis of it, and write it down to track progress.

This incentive reinforced a highly desired behavior in the older two. Our oldest now had a mission, and she pursued it wholeheartedly. The first books she chose were the illustrated 100 page, double spaced, larger font *Magic Treehouse* series by Mary Pope Osborne and others like it. She did well, working her way slowly through each, then dutifully providing a synopsis and recording its completion.

A month into the challenge, we were browsing our local Barnes & Noble where we needed to redeem a gift card. She

---

[10] Set whatever price point works for your family.

loves animals, and came across Erin Hunter, the author of youth fantasy epics, featuring clans of dogs, cats, and polar bears. I expressed doubt when she brought her selection to me. It looked a bit advanced and a little scary. She insisted, and we brought it home.

Before we knew it, Baby Girl was devouring non-illustrated, 320 page, normal font books by the half dozen. She soon manifested her genetic predisposition to stay up late into the night absorbed in her reading. No longer were we fighting to get her to engage in reading. We were struggling to get her to turn off the lights.

After eight months, she finished her hundredth chapter book and received her payout. We discussed what counted as "a chapter book" since there was a significant difference between the books she started and ended the challenge with. Ultimately, we decided a book is a book.

The second hundred will not pay because the incentive served its purpose. Her love of reading has become a part of her. Now we make sure to build in frequent enough library visits.

Ironically, now we need to incentivize her to socialize with other kids. Her preference is to bury her nose in a book instead of hanging out with other kids. While money is only one way to reward a behavior, never underestimate its power.

Little Man engaged more with reading too, though he has not bothered to record his books to claim his reward. He prefers the comic style books over the pure text, which needs to give way at some point to more mature books. Wee One is two years behind, but has this same offer available to her when she is ready to read the chapter books of her choosing.

On this vein, each of the children got their own library cards. There are many financial lessons to be learned from such a simple item – a library card bearing each one's name. They have the power to take out up to 30 items at a time – for FREE! There really is not a better price point for unlimited reading materials and DVD rentals.

With the card comes the responsibility for paying attention to when the books are due, and making sure we return or renew each title in a timely fashion. They are accountable for paying any fines for lost or damaged materials. By comparing the cost of buying new on Amazon or at the local bricks and mortar shops, they get the satisfaction of saving their precious funds, while having thousands of items readily available to them for their personal entertainment.

Personal Electronics

Gizmos

After learning they have the freedom to use their spending accounts, the middle one immediately asked how much a phone costs. I told him it can be as low as $300, but that the service fee is $25 per month. Furthermore, we parents were not yet ready for our children to have phones given their ages.

He then switched his eyes toward an iPad, believing that once he owned any of these magnificent personal electronics that he would have free rein over them.

We corrected that belief immediately, making it clear that even if he bought them, and paid for the ongoing service, he still was under the same restrictions on overall screen time and content as with the family-provided options. It took a bit of wind out of his sails.

In lieu of phones, the girls decided they wanted Gizmo Watches. A Gizmo is a GPS-enabled kid smart watch that can call three pre-programmed phone numbers, while offering some other fun bells and whistles.

At the time, at full price, Gizmos cost about $180 from Verizon plus a $5/month service plan. They're made for younger kids to whom you're not yet willing to entrust a phone but want to keep tabs on.

The GPS lets the parents know where their kid's watch is at any given point in time, enabling two-way communication. It lets you send your kid off on their own without wondering whether they made it to their destination safely. Meanwhile, the kids feel sophisticated.

The kids saw friends with them and wanted one too. One concern is that if we paid for them, they would not appreciate the Gizmo's value and care for it. As this would be the gateway electronic into pricier personal electronics, we wanted to set the stage properly up front.

We agreed with the children that they could buy the Gizmo, and we would cover the monthly service fee. We controlled which three phone numbers were programmed.

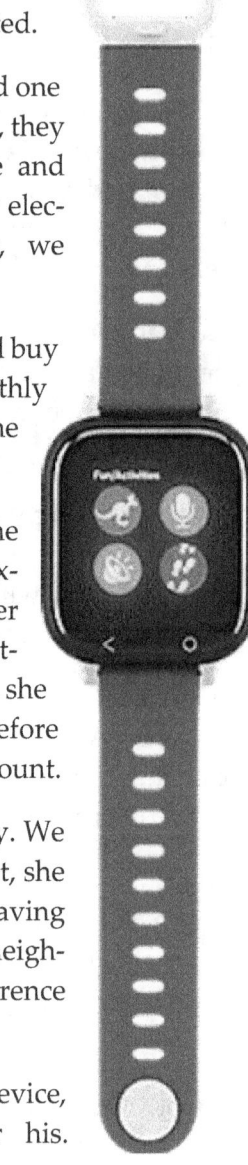

The oldest set her sights on getting one. She packed her lunch religiously, making the exception to buy on French Toast day. After months of hoarding her allowance, pet sitting, and protecting her spending account, she had enough. She waited a few weeks before purchasing, to avoid fully draining her account.

Late June arrived and she was ready to buy. We hit a sale, where for the 2 year commitment, she could get $50 off. Since I didn't see us leaving Verizon Wireless due to reception in our neighborhood, I agreed. $50 makes a huge difference to a kid, and Baby Girl was ecstatic.

We expected that once the oldest had her device, the middle child would save up for his.

Interestingly, it wasn't him but the littlest one who wanted the next Gizmo. She had the advantage of summertime, where there were no lunch purchases to deplete her account. Once she had accumulated enough, she chose a pink Gizmo, also at the discounted rate.

She bought her device in September in time for back to school. Wee One regularly called and texted her three people, and most reliably put it on in the morning. Of the two, the youngest most enthusiastically used her watch until she eventually was given access to a family-provided phone.

Nintendo™ Switch

The kids love video games. Surprising, right?

The middle child had his eyes on a Nintendo™ Switch for a long time. Target had a demo console available to play and he got sidetracked when we passed the electronics department.

I don't love video games, but the bigger idea was to help Little Man learn to save up for something meaningful to him. His initial instinct was to put every $15 he had into new sets of Pokémon™ cards. While we tried not to stand in his way from blowing his allowance on them, we definitely screamed loud objections inside our heads with every booster pack he bought[11]. Getting him onto the idea of saving up for a Switch helped shift his attention.

---

[11] This has been incredibly hard for me to do. I continually toggle between letting him buy as many as he wants (following my own advice) and fighting him on making what I perceive as poor spending decisions.

Initially he thought Switches cost $60, and he was excited when he had enough saved. Imagine his devastation when he learned they cost $300. $60 is the list price for games *after* the console has been bought. Those numbers felt unattainable.

Still, he started saving his lunch money. It was easier in the summer without the lunch line temptations, compounded with birthday money he received. He talked about the Switch, he dreamed about the Switch, he watched videos about the Switch. He was obsessed.

He realized there may be an alternate path. He noticed that his sisters also had money, and that they also like to play video games. We had been talking about school supplies, when the kids shared their plan.

> Mom: *"You're going to have to use some of your money to buy a new ruler that could have gone to a Nintendo™ Switch. Bummer."*
>
> BG: *"He already has enough money to buy a Nintendo™ Switch, because we're splitting the money so it can be both of ours. I'm paying $150, and he is paying $150."*
>
> MP[12]: *"It costs $300? You guys want a toy so bad that you're spending $300?"*
>
> LM: *"It's a video game."*

---

[12] MP is our own Mary Poppins, who adopted our family years ago. She regularly looks after the littles and is our bonus [young] family grandma.

BG: "It's a fun game!"

LM: "But we need to save money to get the games too."

MP: "And how much do they cost?"

LM: "Eh, about $5 each"

MP: "Are you sure? I think they're probably more."

Mom: "Do you remember when you went to Game Stop and you bought used games?

LM: "Mmhmm."

Mom: "Did they work as well as the new game?"

LM: "Yes."

Mom: "Did you care if it was used?"

LM: "I didn't care."

Mom: "Exactly! Was that a good idea to buy a used video game instead of a new game?"

LM: "uh huh."

Mom: "Did it work the same?"

LM: "uh huh."

Mom: "Did it save you a lot of money?"

LM: "uh huh."

Mom: "You can use the money for other things?"

LM: "uh huh."

With a stroke of genius, Little Man negotiated with his big sister to go halfsies on the console and on one game. Switches have two controllers, and she agreed.

Why This is HUGE:

1. Siblings collaborating toward a common goal

2. Independent negotiation skills

3. Problem solving

At the end, she didn't have quite enough to make up her half, but they didn't want to wait an extra week. Per policy, the **First Lennon Bank** doesn't make loans yet, but there's no reason that the children cannot negotiate amongst themselves. Little Man agreed to loan Baby Girl the difference interest-free (his decision). She repaid him a week later from her allowance, going without purchased school lunches to be able to make up the difference. Nowhere in this discussion did parents get involved, and we all were satisfied with the outcome.

They still need to stay within their screen time limits, but the children have added to their fleet of electronic devices through their own actions. They have skin in the game of keeping the devices in working condition, and the pride of having saved for and met a goal.

The children would go on to buy laptops for themselves to play Minecraft and Roblox. The girls bought new (lower end) ones from Amazon, and Little Man bought one of Husband's used higher end computers at half price. Overall screentime limits still apply, regardless of how many electronics the children accumulate.

As they grew, the kids noticed they could earn in-game credits, but they could also buy advantages in their online games for real money. This of course was the faster route to the avatars, costumes, and other in-game purchases. We had to set spending limits to prevent them from going crazy with online gaming purchases.

We initially agreed upon a $5/month limit. They could buy on a monthly basis, or save up a few months to get better bulk pricing. They also started asking for gaming gift cards for birthdays and holidays, seeing this as a short cut to faster online purchasing power.

As each kid grows, their interests and spending guardrails have and will continue to evolve over time.

Rethinking Purchases

At eight years old, Little Man had a new favorite book series, *The Last Kids on Earth* by Max Brallier. What's not to love about the last four kids on earth fighting zombies and a large, intelligent monster named Blarg?

Encouraging the love of reading, I bought him the first book in the series. I had it autographed and delivered to his classroom for the author's visit at school. I figured we could borrow the rest of the series from the library.

Two weeks later, while waiting for our table at a restaurant we stopped into Books a Million across the street. The library was closed and I wanted a vintage Encyclopedia Brown paperback to read together before bed.

Little Man spotted a Max Brallier display of hardbacks, and *had* to get the latest edition. I asked if he really wanted to pay full price for a hardback, and if we should go to the library instead. He insisted on spending his money on it. I said, "OK," and we bought both a copy of Last Kids Book 5 and the Encyclopedia Brown paperback I wanted.

Our table pager buzzed, and we went to dinner. While waiting for our meal, I glanced at the receipt and noticed that we'd been overcharged by $1. I pointed it out to my son, and we decided to go back to get our dollar back. Quick lesson there was to pay attention when ringing up the order, but also not to be afraid to make it right.

After settling the dinner check, we walked back across the street and showed the cashier the error. She confirmed that we were overcharged and issued the refund. After we resolved the Encyclopedia Brown issue, Little Man decided he wanted to return his hardback. Surprised, I asked if he was sure. He confirmed and said he would get it from the library later. Once more, I said, "OK." The cashier gracefully refunded that charge too.

Heading back to the car, I gently probed on his thought process.

> Mom: *"Why did you decide you don't want your book?"*
>
> Little Man: *"So we can buy the Eevee game."*
>
> Mom: *"You don't have a lot of money left?"*
>
> LM: *"But that will give me less money."*
>
> Mom: *"Oh. Do you know where the rest of your money has been going?"*
>
> LM: *"Lunch."*
>
> Mom: *"Know how much you've spent this year?"*
>
> LM: *"No."*
>
> Mom: *"It's about $50. What could you do with $50 if you hadn't bought so many lunches?"*
>
> LM: *"Pokémon."*
>
> Mom: *"Yeah! You could be buying lots of other stuff, but you bought lunch, right. Was it worth it?"*
>
> LM: *"No."*
>
> Mom: *"No? Will you do anything differently?"*
>
> LM: *"Buy less lunch."*

I asked him what he's going to save up for after he buys his Eevee game (for the Nintendo™ Switch) and whether he would start buying lunches again. He said he wanted to save up for something else, but he wasn't sure what. He was starting to connect the dots.

In a different example, it only took a few months until Baby Girl became disappointed in her Gizmo's limited functionality. It didn't do nearly as much as she wanted it to. She regularly forgot to charge or wear it.

It was too late to return it to the store. She tried to resell her Gizmo to her siblings, but her younger sister had already bought one. Her brother was somewhat interested, but she wouldn't come down from asking for the full purchase price. She learned that used items are not nearly as valuable as new, and depreciation is real.

School Supplies

As Labor Day approached, once more the time came to face the hordes at Target picking out school supplies. Pink folders *without prongs* and red folders *with prongs* and blue binders *with pockets* and … you get the picture.

School supply shopping is exciting for kids. Everything is fresh! School hasn't become a chore yet. They're looking forward to seeing friends they'd missed. New binders, undamaged notebook spirals, sharp pencils and fresh erasers rock.

For parents, school supply shopping often means ignoring several pretty good supplies that litter the house. It reinforces the consumerist culture that we find ourselves living in, where the *things* we have are *so last season*. After that, they get discarded, or clutter the house.

School supplies presented the perfect opportunity to offer the gift of choice.

The scene unfolded as such:

1. Here is your budget.
2. You may buy the new [backpack, lunchbox, earbuds, binders, folders…] or you may pocket the money and use last year's [backpack, lunchbox, earbuds, binders, folders…] and/or you may raid Mom's office supply cupboard for free.
3. Anything in-between is fair game, and upgrades come out of pocket. However, you MUST end up with everything the teachers requested.

The kids wrapped their heads around this idea fairly quickly.

LM: "But we need new notebooks!"

Mom: "You definitely need notebooks because you've written in the old ones."

BG: "We definitely need new crayons and glue."

Mom: "You need new glue. Do you need new crayons? Some of your crayons are only a little bit used."

BG: "But most of mine are used!"

Mom: "Would you rather have the money, or would you rather have new crayons? I'll spend the same money either way. I will give it to you, or I will give it to Target, Walmart, or whomever. It doesn't matter to ME because I am spending the money either way. But it matters to YOU because…"
<long pause while everyone reflected>

LM: *"So there's stuff we will HAVE to buy like glue and notebooks and new pencils and stuff. Will we have to use our supply budget on that?"*

Mom: *"You need to have all the right school supplies at the end. If we find school supplies in my cupboards that we already have, either new or gently used, and you choose to use those, then you don't need to buy new ones. You can save the money."*

LM: *"But you said we need to buy new notebooks."*
<He clearly was obsessed over the notebooks.>

Mom: *"You definitely need new notebooks. You won't get to keep every single dollar unless I have notebooks in the cupboard. You can shop for free from my little store, or you can shop with real money at someone else's store."*

LM: *"But we need new markers, new rulers ..."*

Mom: *"Has your ruler really worn out?"*

LM: *"It broke!"*

Mom: *"Then you need a new ruler, unless we have an extra. How did your ruler break? Did you measure too many things?"*

<General laughter>

After the exchange above, we went into a general discussion about video games, and who wanted to buy what, and how much the game discs cost. We talked about the difference between buying new vs. used games, and how they seemed to work the same, regardless of how much we paid and the condition of the packaging.

A parallel was drawn back to school supplies. The kids set off to examine their markers, crayons, and other possibly reusable items. In addition to the school shopping in the moment, we gave them the option to change their minds. If they decided to reuse something early on and later decided they wanted a new item – they could always buy that thing later. We removed the artificial "now or never" urgency of school supply shopping, since they each had the minimum requirements for showing up on the first day of school.

We could have forced them to reuse supplies that still had life in them. We made the conscious decision not to go that route, because we wanted them to find the upside in this budget discussion. To effect positive change in the long game, this had to be a clear win for our test subjects, not a takeaway.

Here is how it unfolded in Year 1:

Rising Fourth Grader (Baby Girl)

- Reused her backpack from last year (and offered an older backpack to her younger sister)

- Reused her lunchbox and earbuds from last year

- Rummaged in the supplies cupboard for other supplies on-hand

- Price shopped at the store to decide on whether or not to pay the differential between the store brand binder and the name brand binder with the better color. Discovered to her delight that the name brand binder cost $0.17 _less_ than the store brand. Loved using the price checker kiosk

- Pocketed the full allotment, which went straight to her ledger. This helped her afford to buy a half interest in a Nintendo™ Switch in September

Third Grader (Little Man)

- Bought a new backpack he spotted at Costco, priced above the allotted budget. Paid out of pocket for the differential. Loves his backpack – with no regrets. He chose to reuse this new backpack the following school year as well

- Bought upgraded headphones with cool colors from Amazon; paid out of pocket for the differential. Very excited to receive and open the Amazon box which was addressed to him

- Reused his lunchbox from last year

- Found his other supplies in the home cupboard, including the notebooks and ruler

- Didn't pocket any surplus and outlaid $1.84. Happy because he had exactly what he wanted

First Grader (Wee One)

- Reused her sister's backpack from last year

- Reused her Snoopy lunchbox from last year, which was a gift from a dear neighbor. Originally she wanted to buy a new one, but when we didn't buy it right away she forgot about it

- Bought new earbuds, since hers from last year were lost or damaged – stayed on budget

- Rummaged through the cupboard for pre-existing supplies, including sharpening what felt like a million pencils to meet the required number

- Pocketed the full budget, which went straight to her ledger. The unspent funds helped get her over the threshold to be able to afford the Gizmo that she chose to purchase later in the year

All in all, the school supplies experiment was a wild success, and we have repeated this exercise every year since. The children were given reasonable budgets to fulfill their annual lists of office products. Empowered to make their own decisions, each took the path that felt right to them.

As the chief school shopping facilitator, I didn't have to say yes or no, but simply ask how much each item cost and if it was worth spending the [sometimes extra] money or not. I made a point to be very neutral and non-judgmental in asking the questions. Each of the three needed to make his or her own decision to fully internalize the lesson.

Halloween Costumes

I'm a killjoy when it comes to Halloween. Spookiness and horror flicks are NOT my jam. Dressing up doesn't appeal to me, and I was never the kid who started planning my costume in August. I can live without candy, and I get annoyed when I find myself eating it simply because it's there. I may go as Uncle Scrooge someday – it would fit.

My kids aren't much different, except for the candy. For them, candy is a gift from the angels above. It should be eaten in large quantities at every opportunity.

They don't play much dress up throughout the year, and they don't get terribly excited about planning their costumes. As the time was ticking, Little Man and I turned to Siri for ideas. "Siri, what should I be for Halloween" was a fun game to play, and Siri offered many suggestions. When the S'more idea came up, he knew it was the one. S'mores around the firepit are a common family activity, and it held some meaning.

I recently had unwrapped a large painting and kept the packing cardboard. With a bit of elastic stitched onto a spare pillow and adding a brown fleece jacket underneath, he made the best human s'more I'd ever met. Better yet – it was free!

He started hemming and hawing with each time we drove past the Spirit of Halloween store. He didn't want to be anything special, he just wanted to buy *something*. It didn't feel like the right answer. I asked the customary question.

"What's it worth to you?"

I told him I'd budgeted $15 for a costume. He could go with what he already had and pocket $15, or he could buy something premade. He chose the cash. His older sister chose to buy a witch's dress. We borrowed a great hat from a neighbor and grabbed the cinnamon broom from beside the fireplace. His younger sister asked to be a peacock, which I made for her using materials from the craft store. All three were happy.

What made this interesting is that with each opportunity to spend or to pocket the money, the children made situational decisions. Whereas Baby Girl chose to keep a lot of her school supply money and packs her lunches the most, she chose to buy a costume. Little Man overspent on school supplies, but pocketed the whole Halloween fund. Wee One buys a lot of lunches, but doesn't shop much otherwise.

Holiday Shopping

We encourage giving, and the holiday season is an obvious time to use your wealth to benefit others. The kids started buying gifts for one another, using personal money and showing a lot of generosity.

As the holiday season rolled around, we had deliberate discussions with budgets and putting thought into what each sibling would be excited to receive. Baby Girl and I started planning in November.

> Mom: "How are you going to budget for how much to spend on them?"
>
> Baby Girl: "I'm not going to spend a whole lot of money. Together I want to spend about $25."
>
> Mom: "That sounds reasonable. It's a little more than half a month's income. What do you think they'll like?"

> BG: "I have a book where you dress up kitties in it with stickers. Wee One adored it, so I'd like to find a book like that for her. Or maybe I'll get her Snoopy related things. She loves Snoopy."

I was happy to hear that she set a reasonable budget relative to her income, and that she focused on what kinds of gifts her siblings would enjoy. She required no nudging, and gave willingly from the heart.

Over the next few years, Baby Girl's budget has increased, as she tries very hard to find the perfect gift for each person. She has a wide circle of people she gifts to.

All three engage in making and buying gifts for others, and they are as excited to buy and wrap as they are to watch their recipient open the gift. Little Man almost emptied his account one year with gift giving, but he accommodated by reducing his spending early in the following year.

A Pandemic and Subsequent Years

The first year (2019) was a resounding success. 2020-2023 brought new twists, between everyone being older … and an unexpected global pandemic. Some of the impacts on the **Lennon Family Bank** included:

- ✎ School lunches stopped when everyone was at home, then were free for the next two years. Forced tradeoffs between French Toast sticks and Pokémon™ cards were no longer relevant.

- ✎ The pool was closed, then restricted, eliminating the lemonade stand opportunity for two years.

- ✎ Fewer people traveled for a while, reducing requests for neighborhood pet sitting jobs. Since then, travel and pet sitting requests have rebounded in full force. Baby Girl opened her own LLC and business bank account in mid-2023.

- ✎ They had extra spending money for use on family vacations and BSA scout camping trips.

- ✎ They loaned money between themselves, sometimes with interest, sometimes without.

- ✎ Between buying and being gifted fish supplies, each now maintains an aquarium in their room. They are learning that pets can be expensive as well as enjoyable.

❧ Little Man has taken up an interest in WWE wrestling. He started setting aside a portion of his spending account to start a Wrestlemania fund. The 2024 event is in Philadelphia, which is a several hour drive from our home. His savings goal is $500 to help cover admission and lodging.

❧ Four years later, they have each been given use of family-owned cell phones. While we bought the phones (they belong to us) and pay for ongoing service, the kids have bought cases and apps. If any loses or breaks the phone, they are responsible for its replacement. If they choose to upgrade at some point, it's on their dime.

Indeed, Little Man recently took his phone swimming. As of publication, he is exploring options for replacing the device including saving up his allowance, doing work for Dad, largely recycling last year's school supplies, and selling a used Beverly Cleary book set in our neighborhood online classifieds.

❧ They started doing occasional work for and getting paid by Husband's business. This active income will trigger official 2023 1099-NEC forms, allowing them to file income taxes next year, and contribute to Roth IRAs. Understanding that time is on their side, the more they can contribute while they're young, the greater their nest eggs will be when the time comes to use it.

❧ We opened First Banking accounts, transferring their spending ledgers into Chase Bank. These accounts come with Debit Cards (they are thrilled), and an app that lets them track their balances real time on their phones. Allowance payments are now automated transfers.

ॐ Baby Girl decided to self-publish a cookbook on Amazon. This includes selecting, testing, updating, photographing, and typing out recipes, then going through the self-publishing process on Amazon KDP. She'll need to learn how to market and advertise her book, earning a small perpetual revenue stream of royalties in return.

PREVIEWS OF CONVERSATIONS YET TO COME

Year One saw many interesting conversations and new behaviors. Years Two through Four showed continual growth and understanding of how money works. The next several years will see continued growth as we foray into new topics. Here are several we have teed up.

Family Travel Planning

Our travel plans were solidified going into Year One, and the Pandemic put the kibosh on travel for the next two years. Now we can finally engage the whole family in detailed vacation planning.

I belong to many online money discussion forums. I often see threads debating the tradeoff between not wanting to spend money vs. wanting to travel as a family.

Travel *can* be expensive, but it doesn't *have* to break the bank. Without going into all the options of staying with friends or family, house hacking, home swapping, credit card point optimization, tax deductible "workations," or medical tourism, we will focus on what will benefit the kids most in learning how to budget and plan for travel.

Most kids love travel. It breaks the monotony, and planes, trains, and hotels are awesome. They don't see the hassle, germs, or expense. When you overlay the magnificence of sandy beaches or Disney, game over.

This costs money. To reinforce the abundance mindset, we can put everyone's creativity to work toward solutions, while illustrating **the problem statement**.

- **Part 1**: the family wants to go somewhere and do something.

- **Part 2:** at any given point in time, money [and time] may be more or less available for travel

Perhaps you've set a budget for travel (good job!), but it's not likely to involve the Ritz Carlton and first class airfare. Financial constraints are real, as are school year calendars and the ability to take time off at the office.

We want to get the kids involved in the decision making process of how to optimize our travel funds. We'll spend the budget one way or another. The more they influence how we spend it, the more they'll get out of each trip, and the more they'll enjoy it. For a detailed example, please see page 92.

Investing their Savings – and Giving it to Them

We need to start looking at the savings accounts they have been building. After four years, each has accumulated at least $2500. Rather than Husband and me continuing to pay them the interest on this account, it's in our shared interest to have the money grow externally.

Investments such as Vanguard low-load index funds are a great way to introduce them to the ups and downs of the US stock market.[13] They can watch their portfolio movement online and will receive a monthly statement.

A word of caution – account titling matters. As of now, these savings and investment accounts will remain joint with us, as we want to wait and assess maturity level of each as they get closer to age 18.

You'll need to talk to your favorite tax and financial advisors to decide whether you'll want to set up UGMA (Uniform Gifts to Minors Act) accounts and if so, when. UGMAs come with pros and cons, notably tied to college financial aid eligibility, tax rates, and control over the funds, all of which is very family-specific. The Lennons tend to prefer to retain control until we are confident in each child's readiness for the freedom and privileges large sums of money offer.

If you don't set up an UGMA, you'll need to keep an eye on the balance you're accumulating (that the kids believe is their money, but as minors it technically isn't) vs. the current gift tax threshold. You'll need to gift it to them at some point. As of 2023, the annual IRS gift tax exclusion amount is $17,000.

This exclusion is:
- the amount an individual can gift
- to any one person
- each year
- free of any tax implications.

---

[13] Vanguard isn't paying me to promote them; I'm simply a fan and I put my money where my mouth is.

If you are working with another parent, you each have a gift tax exclusion. The pair of you could gift twice the threshold (e.g., $34,000 in 2023) to little Taylor. If little Taylor's balance exceeds the gift tax exclusion, consider splitting your gifting between different tax years.

Talk to your favorite tax person for tailored tax advice, because I'm not her. Please don't incur a gift tax burden when the time comes to hand over the nest egg they've been working hard to build over the years.

Extending Credit in Both Directions

As noted above, when we first launched our Family Bank, the children were not allowed to spend more money than they had on their spending ledgers.

Per Statista.com's recent survey of 161 countries on credit card penetration, the US is #9 in the world with 66.7% of individuals 15+ years old owning one or more credit cards.[14] Given the hundreds of millions of cards issued in the US, most US cardholders have several pieces of plastic in their wallets.

Americans love to buy on credit. It can be a great tool if you pay your balance in full each billing cycle, and perhaps gain some cash or travel rewards. It can be terrible if you revolve the debt from month to month, paying financing fees and potentially falling behind or getting in over your head. We need

---

[14] Canada is the highest (82.7%), followed by Israel (79.1%), and Iceland (74%).
Source: https://www.statista.com/statistics/675371/ownership-of-credit-cards-globally-by-country/ accessed 4/3/2023

to make sure the kids are able to handle credit before extending it.

I spent eight years working for a major US credit card issuer. My head exploded when I learned how many people got credit cards, not understanding that they were required to pay back the money. Where is the financial literacy in our country? Schools are starting to lean into teaching finance basics, but we're woefully late to the game.

Our intention is that the children learn how credit works before they use it. They will learn about contracts, and if they take out a loan, there will be a promissory note laying out the exact terms and conditions. If they fail to honor their commitments, there will be consequences.

Our friends did exactly this when their teenage daughter wanted a car. Written into the contract was a requirement that she keep the vehicle clean and tidy. At some point, she stopped tending to the car's hygiene. When her keys went missing, she was beside herself trying to find them as she was getting increasingly late for school.

Finally, she asked if her dad knew where her keys were.

"Yes, I have them," he simply replied.

 Flabbergasted, she asked for them back and when he refused, asked how she was supposed to get to school.

Shrugging, he let her know that was her problem to solve. She had failed to live up to her contractual obligations; the consequences were exactly as laid out in their agreement.

The life lesson he taught her was that paperwork, contracts, and commitments matter. She had the great fortune to have a teachable moment in a very safe setting. So many others get in trouble with very disinterested lenders, who enforce their contracts without a loving hand to steer their borrowers back onto the right path.

On the flip side, we're happy to borrow their money, put it to good use, and pay them interest on it. There will be written paperwork outlining the terms of the loan, and they'll get to learn what it means to be a lender.

Earned Income and Funding Roth IRAs

Our family loves the idea of early investing and tax-free growth. The Roth IRA is a gift from Congress to allow us to build wealth tax free. The children have time on their side when it comes to the power of compounding. The more we can help them get earnings into Roth IRAs, the better off financially they will be later.

There is an extra benefit to establishing and funding the Roth IRA early. After the account has seasoned for five years, even if you're younger than 59½ years old, you can make a tax-free withdrawal of up to $10,000[15] to help pay for a first-time home purchase.

The cleanest way to put money into Roths are with earned income backed by employer tax filings. Husband's company has many opportunities for the children to get involved. Others in

---

[15] Allowable limit as of 2023

his industry are willing and able to employ minors in a wide variety of functions where they can add value; it's not just a family affair.

Another plan is to ask the neighbors who employ Baby Girl for pet care to submit 1099s for her. We will pre-fill the forms to make it easy for them to file (and it costs the neighbors nothing). The goal is for her to report that income on her taxes with appropriate, legal substantiation of her earned income so it is eligible for her Roth IRA. She formed her LLC and opened a business bank account in mid-2023 to further support the tracking of her earned income.

Once the IRA is funded, then it's about how to grow that money, whether through low load index funds or other traditional or non-traditional investment choices.

In Conclusion... and Looking Ahead

After four years of fostering financial literacy within the Lennon household, we concluded that this simple program was a raging success. Key wins include:

- All three children better understand money and how to make financial tradeoffs

- Husband and I have more help around the house. We don't pack school lunches anymore

- Giving money to our children doesn't cost much. We already budget for certain expenditures; they participate in deciding where the money goes

- We say fewer Nos. The children decide how to allocate money to things they care about

- The children exhibit new skills including collaboration, negotiation, problem solving, and initiative to drum up business

- We are building the foundation for future conversations.

Our goal is that when our children leave the nest, they are exceptionally capable of managing their finances. Each will know how to earn an income based on skills and assets they have, and how to budget to meet their financial and lifestyle goals.

They will understand how to save wisely and to spend wisely. They will have strong executive functions to delay gratification in order to reach larger goals – financial and otherwise.

Taxes and retirement savings will simply be a way of life. They will learn how to win at these games within the provisions of the tax code, including investments in Roth retirement vehicles to the full extent possible.

We want our children to understand and enjoy their money. When it's plentiful, it's fun and more a source of joy than of stress. I've even heard it described as the universal religion.

> "Money is the most universal and most efficient system of mutual trust ever devised. Even people who do not believe in the same god or obey the same king are more than willing to use the same money. Osama bin-Laden, for all his hatred of American culture, American religion, and American politics, was very fond of American dollars."
> ~ Yuval Noah Harari, Sapiens

Looking ahead, we have several years of continued reinforcement. Earning, saving, and spending money will never go out of style. As they get into their teenage years, we will give them new financial learning opportunities.

In a few years, they each will be facing larger expenses. We may start extending credit. They will be able to take out a loan if the purchase feels manageable. They will learn about contracts and the consequences of breaching them. How's that for teeing up a sequel!

Eventually each will get credit cards and will need to understand how they work. They will build their credit one piece at a time, and avoid getting buried in consumer debt.

A key to success is knowing how to use and control money, so it doesn't control you. The more you allow your children control over making money decisions early in their life, the greater their skills at managing this constrained resource will be. This gift to our children will serve them a lifetime. My hope is that you can pass on this same legacy of financial literacy to your family.

Resources

Online

Free downloads: www.MagnifiYourLife.com/resources/

Teaching Guide

When I shared an early version of this methodology with another mama friend, she was interested in the framework, but worried about teaching her kids these concepts on top of everything else she was working on with them. Inspired, I took it upon myself to do a bit of the direct teaching.

Check out **GoldQuest** – a story for your children to enjoy. 12-year-old twins Buck and Penny find themselves trapped inside their video game. They must figure out how to get back home, which can only be done by learning the ins and outs of earning, saving, and spending in their video game world – ultimately mastering their scoreboards.

GoldQuest is available on Amazon. Encourage your

children to read it, then use the discussion questions at the end to foster dinner table conversations.

Detailed Travel Planning Example

Four strategies for traveling (and engaging the kids in the process) offer varying levels of excitement, involvement, and negotiation.

Strategy 1: Go nowhere and save the money

Pro: Money isn't spent.

Cons: It's boring and you miss out on the excitement of travel. This defeats the purpose, which is to figure out how to engage your family with more travel, while staying within a designated budget.

Strategy 2: Plan the trip and make it sound awesome

You want to avoid explaining why Hawaii isn't in the budget and that your kids can go there when they're paying for it. Whatever you plan and do pales in comparison once they've set their sights on the jet setting life, if they have no understanding or appreciation for how quickly travel budgets can be eaten up.

Pros: You retain full control of the trip. You contain the expenses.

With luck, the kids are satisfied with their experiences.

The success of this is often inversely proportionate to how old they are. The younger, the better.

Cons: As children get older, they start to be more aware of what other families do. Once they get a taste for travel, they start wanting more variety and more of what little Johnny Jones next door gets to do.

"But Johnny's family is going to Hawaii!! Why can't we? It's not fair!"

Strategy 3: You set the budget, let the kids plan

Pros: The kids get to see the constraints and be part of the solution. They get to research their options and go through the pricing exercise. They start weighing tradeoffs on their own.

They can weigh the activities vs. cost and duration and make decisions. When they own the decisions, they enjoy the results more and can't fuss about what they're not getting to do.

Cons: What they choose to do may not be your first choice. I recommend that you go with it anyway, to respect the process and give them a chance to contribute to the family's plans.

Plus, if they plan it, they have nothing to complain about. The trip may be more peaceful than usual.

Strategy 4: Kids add skin in the game ($)

In this strategy, the children pony up an age-appropriate contribution to the trip budget. What's age-appropriate will vary from family to family, based on the kids normal earning, saving, and spending patterns.

I suggest you choose an amount that the children will feel, but not be devastated by. Maybe it's half to two thirds of their spending money for a few months. They can still spend here and there, but they have to be extra thoughtful, since they have less than usual.

Don't cripple their spending forever, because their attention spans aren't that long yet. Expecting too much delayed gratification is setting everyone up for failure. By setting a target and having ongoing conversations about their goal provides meaning for their sacrifice with anticipation of a fabulous adventure.

During the trip itself, you can earmark that activity X is paid for by Payton or Taylor. As with strategy 3, have your child price out how the family will spend it. They will understand how far their dollars go. Have them give the cashier the payment. The whole family should make a point to thank the sponsoring child profusely for the adventure they allowed the family to do. Reinforce how you wouldn't otherwise be able to enjoy that family event without their contributions. Make it a big deal.

Pros: Skin in the game for the kids. If they want to go to Hawaii, ensure they feel enough of the sacrifice and recognize this isn't an every year event. They will feel the sacrifice and the satisfaction of knowing they enabled the family to do something out of the ordinary.

The next time they want an expensive activity, they will weigh what sacrifice they are willing to make, facilitating a more productive conversation.

Cons: If they're willing to sacrifice meaningfully to make this trip happen, you must be prepared to make sacrifices too.

Don't put this option out there if you're not willing to follow through or you'll teach a different lesson entirely.

Case Study:

While on a business training trip, we called home. The oldest started applying pressure for us to come home early, and I responded that we still had two days of class. I also told her we hope to start bringing them with us on future trips. She immediately started asking to return to Disney World, which we visited two years prior.

I asked her if she was ready to pay for it, as Husband loudly discouraged me from committing to anything. We've talked about going back next year, but had already made plans for a camping trip this summer based on their input.

This is the opening to discuss what your family values in a vacation. Do you want full Disney immersion? Is a pool part of your plan for any non-park down days? Will you eat out?

Key variables may include:

- Transportation to and at the destination
- Accommodations for sleeping, eating, and downtime in-between adventures
- Admissions (multi-day pass, alternate between the parks, a pool/beach, or other destinations)
- Tradeoffs of trip duration, off-season dates, and how long everyone is willing to save up for it.

I asked Baby Girl where she wants to sleep: at a hotel, at a friend's, or in our car. She picked the first, because hotels are more fun. She asked how much they cost. Prices vary wildly, from low budget off-premise hotels to top of the line on-resort accommodations. I told her that they range from $200-$1000 per night and asked her how many nights she wanted to stay. It was a softball opportunity for her to do some simple math.

She decided she wanted to stay a week and set about to calculate the cost. This was the beginning of a conversation and a negotiation. I never told her it was too expensive, I simply let her figure out how much it would be.

I found that a typical 7 day trip to Disney/Orlando in early December for a family of 5 could range from $4,785 to $12,890 and up[16]. That's quite a spread; it doesn't include fast passes.

If we had local friends with a guest room, had hotel points to use, or were willing to stay at less-frills hotels, then the lodging price could drop further. Our challenge is that hotel rooms for five people are hard to find, without getting two rooms and skyrocketing the cost. Airbnbs often are our best option.

On the other hand, if we wanted to maximize the Disney experience, that price would continue to climb. It's about making intentional choices.

---

[16] Originating in central VA, as priced online in May, 2023

Age-Appropriate Family Responsibility Ideas

Responsibilities for children ages 2 to 3

- Assist in straightening their bed covers
- Put dirty clothes in laundry basket
- Put away toys and books into specified bins
- Fill pet's food dish/water bowl
- Wipe up spills
- Push a Swiffer™ (minus an extension) around the floor

Responsibilities for children ages 4 to 5

Any of the above responsibilities, plus:

- Make bed, clear out everything from underneath
- Empty wastebaskets
- Sort dirty laundry by color
- Match socks after they are washed
- Vacuum a room (adult will need to plug in)
- Use hand-held vacuum to pick up crumbs
- Make sure each bathroom has spare toilet paper
- Set / clear the table with supervision
- Bring in mail or newspaper
- Unload utensils from dishwasher

Responsibilities for children ages 6 to 7

Any of the above responsibilities, plus:

- Keep bedroom tidy
- Sort and put away clean laundry
- Set and clear table
- Fix bowl of cereal
- Help make and pack school lunches
- Be responsible for feeding a pet daily
- Sweep floors
- Water houseplants
- Water garden; Help weed the garden and plant new seedlings (with supervision)

Responsibilities for children ages 8 to 9

Any of the above responsibilities, plus:

- Put groceries away
- Make own breakfast, snacks; help make dinner
- Load dishwasher; wipe table after meals
- Wipe down kitchen and bathroom counters
- Mop floor, Vacuum unassisted
- Sort, Fold, and Put away own laundry
- Bring empty trash/recycling bins from curb
- Take smaller dogs for a walk
- Pick up/dispose of animal waste in the yard
- Scoop cat litter box

Responsibilities for children ages 10 to 12

Any of the above responsibilities, plus:

- Be responsible for own homework
- Take full trash/recycling to the curb for pick-up
- Do own laundry from start to finish
- Change & launder their own bed sheets
- Cook simple meal with supervision
- Unload dishwasher; Clean kitchen
- Clean hardwood stairs (damp cloth) or carpeted stairs (small handheld vacuum)
- Rake yard leaves; weed garden beds
- Wash windows, clean mirrors
- Take larger dogs for a walk
- Baby-sit younger siblings (with adult nearby)

Responsibilities for children ages 13 and older

Any of the above responsibilities, plus:

- Clean bathroom incl. toilets (inside and out)
- Wash and vacuum cars
- Tutor younger siblings
- Baby-sit younger siblings on their own
- Mow lawn
- Help more deeply in the family business

☙ · ❧

Age-Appropriate Kidpreneur Ideas

Income ideas for kids 4-5

- Provide modeling services for family's/friend's small business marketing materials
- Stuff/Seal/Stamp envelopes
- Collect cans or bottles in states with deposits

Income ideas for kids 6-7

Any of the above ideas, plus:

- Lemonade / Hot Cocoa / Cookie stands
- Pull weeds, collect acorns / gumballs, other simple yardwork
- Offer bonus earning challenges around the house beyond routinely expected chores

Income ideas for kids 8-9

Any of the above ideas, plus:

- Dog walking and/or pet sitting while neighbors are away from home
- Make and sell bird houses, bath bombs, goat milk soap, or other handmade items
- Start vegetable or flower seedlings; sell to neighbors for their gardens or at a yard sale
- Sell outgrown clothes / books / toys at a yard sale
- Set up a fitness or a reading challenge (see page 54 for ideas)

Income ideas for kids 10+

Any of the above ideas, plus:

- Perform odd jobs/yardwork for neighbors or family
  - Snow Shoveling
  - Helping elderly neighbors sweep their front walk
  - Mulching is a popular task for adults to outsource, though due to weight they may need to put the bags near their destination
  - A neighbor recently posted a $20 job offer for a kid to dig a 2' x 2' hole. Never know what someone will need if you don't ask
- Write and illustrate a book; self-publish on Amazon's KDP with Mom & Dad's help
- Provide tutoring to younger neighbor children
- Offer sports technique coaching for younger neighbor children
- Babysit / watch young kids at a large gathering so the parents can socialize with one another
- Higher responsibility / value-add participation in your family's business ventures (yours, your siblings', your parents', your close friends', etc.)

❧ · ☙

ACKNOWLEDGEMENTS

Special thanks to my children, who are the cheerful guinea pigs in this financial experiment. Hopefully they will look back appreciatively as they apply these same principles to their own kids down the line.

I would be remiss if I did not acknowledge my parents, who imposed the *Brooks Bank* upon my sister and me. We admittedly hated it … until we each got to college in the early 1990s and had a nice chunk of change to spend. It eased a lot of the financial crunches our peers had to deal with, and we knew we'd earned that money. It wasn't a handout; we treated it with the appropriate respect. Mom and Dad taught us how to save and spend, delay gratification (albeit grudgingly), and understand that not every dollar we earned was ours to keep.

Lastly, my deepest respect and admiration to Dear Husband who is as passionate as I about teaching our children how to handle their personal finances from the beginning. We negotiated ourselves onto the same page, and stand in solidarity to teach the children habits for a lifetime of success. Thou.

ABOUT THE AUTHOR

Stephanie married her high school crush and lives in Richmond, Virginia with the love of her life, their three young children, two cats, and a rescue pup. She is passionate about personal growth, holistic health, real estate, achieving financial independence, and showing her children the world. She publishes under both Stephanie Lennon and Brooke Lennon.

Engage with Stephanie:

Explore: www.MagnifiYourLife.com

Follow: Facebook @MagnifiYourLife

Tiktok @ MagnifiYourLife

Instagram @ MagnifiYourLife

Write: Stephanie@ MagnifiYourLife.com